CHAT GPT &
SOCIAL MEDIA
MARKETING

RYAN TURNER

SUMMARY

INTRODUCTION

In the fast-paced modern world of marketing, it is increasingly important to keep up with the times and find new ways to stand out from the competition.

As technology continues to evolve, the tools and strategies available to marketers must also adapt to changes and innovations. Among the ocean of innovations that have crowded the world, there is one technology that has gained prominence in recent years: it is artificial intelligence, also known as AI.

Artificial intelligence has emerged as a powerful tool for marketers, offering a range of benefits and possibilities that were previously not even imaginable. Among the programs based on this technology, ChatGPT, a free open-source artificial intelligence capable of interacting in a manner extremely similar to that of a human being, has made its mark. This innovation is increasingly opening the door to a world in which human-machine collaboration is possible even in typically creative fields such as marketing.

This book was created to provide a tool for all marketing professionals who want to stay ahead of the curve and understand the potential of artificial intelligence. In the course of this handbook, we will discover what artificial intelligence and ChatGPT are, how they work, and what to do to set them up and customize them for your business.

Next, we will explore the world of marketing and how artificial intelligence can be leveraged to improve performance and customer relationships. From automating tasks to optimizing communication strategies to measuring the effectiveness of a campaign, we will cover everything you need to integrate your marketing plan with artificial intelligence.

We will also delve into the social media channel, which is increasingly important for creating effective communication, and provide you with practical tips for implementing AI in the creation of increasingly personalized content.

Finally, we will examine how the future of marketing will change due to the evolution and increasing application of artificial intelligence in this field.

Whether you are a marketing professional new to artificial intelligence or a seasoned practitioner looking to explore this topic further, this book will provide you with all the information you need to make the most of AI's potential.

1.
LEARN ABOUT ARTIFICIAL INTELLIGENCE AND CHATGPT

WHAT IS ARTIFICIAL INTELLIGENCE?

Artificial intelligence, also called AI, denotes a technological tool endowed with typically human capabilities such as learning, creativity, reasoning and planning.

Although artificial intelligence has existed for more than fifty years, it is only in the last few decades that great achievements have been made. This is due to rapid technological evolution, the immense amount of data available and the creation of new, highly advanced algorithms.

To better understand the scope of this tool, suffice it to say that this type of technology is so advanced that it is capable of understanding its environment, relating to what it perceives around it, solving any problems, and taking action to achieve a set goal.

In essence, the machine works just like the human brain: it receives data, processes it and reacts accordingly. And, just like the human mind, AI is able to modify its behavior based on experience and analysis of previous actions.

WHAT IS CHATGPT?

ChatGPT, an acronym for the English words *Chat Generative Pre-trained Transformer*, is an artificial intelligence-based chatbot prototype developed by OpenAI. Today it represents one of the most effective tools in the world because of its ability to generate texts that are almost identical to those made by a human being in any language in the world.

Initially it was developed to support some simple tasks such as generating text, making translations, and answering general questions. Over time, however, ChatGPT has also found use in more business-related contexts such as customer service or sales.

This new declination of the model is due to its very nature, which is designed to create dialogues and conversations based on natural and human language. Thanks to the amount of data available online, the model has been trained on the basis of texts on the Internet, thus learning to generate human responses to questions or requests of all kinds. Currently, ChatGPT can be used to generate messages, conversations, emails, chatbots or other types of texts.

The model consists of several layers of neurons specialized in text analysis and processing. Each layer is responsible for recognizing specific features such as word meaning, grammatical structure, or relationship to context. This sophisticated structure allows the model to respond naturally and consistently to any query made.

As you can easily guess, its incredible versatility makes ChatGPT an expendable tool in countless areas and circumstances. For example, it can be harnessed to create chatbots capable of automatically answering customer questions, or to devise engaging posts useful for intriguing potential customers on social media. It also finds application in the creation of more detailed content such as articles or blog posts.

Despite the positive qualities and incredible potentials of this artificial intelligence-based tool, it is worth noting one overriding point. Unlike the human mind, in fact, ChatGPT is not (yet) equipped with a conscience or ethics. This means that the model is not yet able to distinguish between appropriate and inappropriate content, thus leaving open the possibility of creating unethical content.

Should you wish to integrate ChatGPT into your enterprise, it is therefore essential that the texts be checked and moderated by humans.

EXAMPLES FOR INTEGRATING CHATGPT IN THE ENTERPRISE

ChatGPT is an extremely powerful tool because of its ability to generate models that can be used in the NLP field, that is, in natural language processing.

Among the most common modes of use of ChatGPT we find:

- Text generation
  ChatGPT can be used to generate consistent, fluent text on an infinite variety of topics. This makes the template an extremely effective tool for writers, marketing managers and other professionals who need to create high-quality text on a regular basis.

- Chatbot development
  ChatGPT can be calibrated to mimic the writing style of a specific group or subject, a quality that makes it perfect for developing chatbots that can converse with users in a natural way that is almost identical to that of a human being.

- Translations

  ChatGPT can be trained so that it is capable in performing language translations from any language The model can even work on multiple translations in parallel to translate a single text into multiple languages.

- Summaries

  ChatGPT can be used to summarize more complex or articulate texts. In this case it can be calibrated against a database of summaries, so that it can learn how to generate summaries from an article, news story, or any other text.

- Answers to questions

  This model can be used to answer questions; to do so, simply train ChatGPT on a dataset of questions and answers so that it generates answers based on the context and the question asked.

- Sentiment analysis

  ChatGPT can be used to analyze the sentiments expressed in a text. For example, it can recognize whether an article expresses concepts with negative, positive, or neutral sentiments.

- Recognition of characters or entities

  ChatGPT has the ability to identify and extract characters or entities such as people, locations, organizations, and so on from text.
- Grammatical analysis

  Another feature of ChatGPT is that it can perform grammatical analysis of the text or a specific sentence. In fact, the model can recognize and distinguish nouns, verbs, or adjectives.

- Understanding of text and language
ChatGPT can be set up to perform a wide variety of tasks related to the language used in a text. For example, it can perform syntactic or semantic analysis.

- Creation of specific texts
Among the most interesting functions of ChatGPT is the ability to generate specific document types such as legal documents, financial reports, articles, posts for social media, and so on.

- Creative writing
ChatGPT can also be used in the field of creative writing, this is because it can write poems, short stories and even scripts. Its ability to generate fluent and coherent text makes it an extremely useful tool for writers looking for inspiration or for all people who need to generate different versions and variations on a text.

- Content writing
In addition to creative writing, ChatGPT also finds application in writing content such as articles, blog posts, or product descriptions. With its ability to understand the context and meaning of text, this model can generate high-quality text on a wide variety of topics.
This incredible quality makes ChatGPT an extremely effective tool in content creation and marketing.

- Posts for social media

From the description of ChatGPT's latest qualities, it is easy to imagine how it can also be leveraged for creating social media-specific posts and content, essential channels for all modern businesses. Specifically, ChatGPT can be set up to automate the creation of content for social media.

- Customer service and emailing
ChatGPT's language capabilities also make it an excellent ally in the area of customer service and email or newsletter delivery. For example, it can generate automated responses for customers who send inquiries through this channel or generate weekly newsletters.

- Coding
ChatGPT, when trained on a code dataset, can even be used in coding. To give a practical example, it can be exploited to automate the writing of repetitive codes.

- Virtual Assistant
This model can even turn into a virtual assistant and perform classic tasks of this job such as scheduling appointments, making reservations or providing information of interest.

- Educational assistant
ChatGPT also finds a role in education in that, if set up in this perspective, it can become a tutor who can provide explanations, answer questions or even devise specific tests or exercises.

- Medical care
If set up in this way, ChatGPT can turn into a medical assistant and thus help doctors during tasks such as

diagnosis, treatment evaluation or communication with patients.

- Data analysis
ChatGPT can easily be trained for data analysis, creation of summaries or specific insights. This function can be implemented in different business areas such as marketing or administration.

- Gaming design
The great potential of ChatGPT means that it can also be used in the gaming sector as the model has the ability to generate stories and dialogues for gaming or create game mechanisms.

The long list just provided provides a broad yet non-exhaustive overview of the many fields of application of ChatGPT in the enterprise and beyond.
Specifically, its ability to generate high-quality texts and perform many different tasks makes this model a valuable ally for professionals and developers in all fields. Functions such as generating texts, creating chatbots, analyzing sentiment, setting up a Facebook post, sending newsletters or analyzing data are all common to most international businesses and are all key building blocks for creating and developing a successful and competitive business in an increasingly fierce market.

REQUIREMENTS FOR USING CHATGPT
In this section we will focus on what are the steps to successfully download ChatGPT.

Before we begin, it is worth noting that there are some requirements that should be present. Specifically:

- Technical Requirements
  In order for ChatGPT to be used properly, certain technical parameters are important. This means that you need a computer with a powerful graphics card and sufficient memory space to run the program.
  In general, it is recommended to use a GPU as it can significantly increase the speed and performance of ChatGPT. In addition, you should use one of the newer versions of Python and download appropriate libraries such as Hugging Face Transformers, a useful site for downloading pre-trained templates capable of solving problems similar to those you are interested in.
- Training data
  This is a fundamental pre-requisite for the use of ChatGPT. Having sufficient quality data available for training increases the likelihood that the model will be trained correctly and thus be able to provide human-like responses.
  To ensure specific and targeted training, it is critical to collect enough data on the market of interest. In addition, it is important that the data be as relevant as possible to the model that will be used.

- Knowledge of programming
  Proper use of ChatGPT's advanced features requires minimal knowledge in programming and technology. This point is nodal to understanding the concepts on which machine learning is based, such as neural network or training processes. Both in fact represent the basis from which a specific model can be developed and adapted.

A basic knowledge of programming, specifically Python, is also recommended.

- Time and resources
  Harnessing the full potential of ChatGPT requires an investment in time and resources, both of which are essential to developing an appropriate model for specific goals. This investment covers key steps such as data collection, training, model optimization, application development, and integration of artificial intelligence within business processes. It follows that it is essential to have sufficient time and resources available to devote to this technology, not only during the implementation phase, but also thereafter. Indeed, to ensure sustained success, it is important to update ChatGPT and ensure that it operates effectively and in step with the times.

As soon as these pre-requisites are met, it will be possible to proceed with the next steps and engage in model development.

In its free version, in order to use the potential of ChatGPT, you just need to go to the appropriate site, namely https://chat.openai.com and register. Once this is done, you will have access to a rather simple interface where you will be able to type in the requests you wish to submit to the artificial intelligence.

In the next chapter, we will focus instead on the advanced set-up of ChatGPT and on customizing the model so that it can perform as well as possible with respect to our needs. Since this is a next step, if your needs are not complex, you can take advantage of the full potential of the free version by registering for the ChatGPT platform.

2.
ADVANCED CHATGPT SET-UP

In this chapter we will focus on the advanced processes required to perform set-up and customization of ChatGPT. As anticipated in the previous chapter, these steps are not mandatory and can be implemented by professionals who wish to have access to more complex features by adapting the model to their specific business needs. If you are not familiar with the technology or have no interest in using the more advanced features, you can skip these steps and simply register with the platform https://chat.openai.com.

Using this technology in its most advanced version requires preparation and configuration of certain tools within the business organization. This relevant topic will be addressed in the following pages, where we will go through step by step what to do to configure the model and how to customize it to your specific needs.

This step includes selecting the necessary hardware and software, preparing the data for training, optimizing the model, and implementing it within business processes. In addition, we will understand how to perform proper maintenance and how to continue training ChatGPT even after its installation.

By following the points in this chapter, you will be able to successfully install ChatGPT in your business, automating processes and improving efficiency.

INSTALL CHATGPT

For ChatGPT to be successfully incorporated into business processes and adapted to internal needs, there are certain steps that must be followed.

- Choice of hardware and software

  The first step toward integrating artificial intelligence requires evaluating and choosing the hardware and software to be used in the process. We have already introduced this concept and know that in order to run ChatGPT properly, a computer with a powerful graphics card, such as a GPU, and a recent version of Python is required. Special libraries and useful tools to improve the functioning of the model are also recommended.

  Beyond these technical features, it is also important to ensure that hardware and software have the minimum requirements required by ChatGPT to provide positive and efficient performance.

- Data collection for training

  A key step in the implementation of ChatGPT is the collection of data with which the model will be trained to perform specific tasks. In general, models are trained on the basis of the much information on the Internet, and it is here that they acquire their ability to generate human-like responses.

  To train your model to meet the specific demands of your industry, it is critical to collect data that is as accurate and clear as possible. In addition, it is important that this data be relevant to the model in which it will be used and to your business goals.

- Model optimization

After preparing the data for the model, the next step requires optimizing the model. This step involves adjusting and modifying ChatGPT parameters so as to improve results and reduce the incidence of errors. At this stage, it is critical to test and validate the model, ensuring that it meets the needs of the business as closely as possible and provides accurate and positive outputs.

- ChatGPT Implementation
The optimization of the personalized model is followed by the actual implementation into business processes. This phase may take on different implications depending on the field of artificial intelligence use: it may decline into the creation of a chatbot, the programming of a virtual assistant or the drafting of a marketing plan. Whatever the purpose of the model, it must be integrated carefully to ensure a stable and secure implementation that does not jeopardize business continuity.

- Maintenance and review
ChatGPT is not a done and done tool. It, just like the markets in which most companies operate, is constantly evolving. This means that review must be ongoing so that action can be taken to improve functionality or fix bugs or other errors.

- Continuous training of the model
This phase is actually closely related to the previous one since effective maintenance absolutely must involve continuous education of the model. As the complexity in natural language processing increases, it becomes essential to regularly update the program and add new training data that can keep ChatGPT up to date. This is an extremely relevant activity to

ensure excellent performance and improve the accuracy of the outputs obtained by artificial intelligence.

As can be seen from the points just addressed, implementing and customizing ChatGPT requires careful planning and precise execution. Do not underestimate any step and be careful when evaluating hardware, software, and preparing data for model training. Don't forget to optimize ChatGPT before incorporating it into your business processes, and keep it continuously updated on the top list of your priorities. Only in this way can you benefit from the full potential of AI.

DATA COLLECTION AND PERSONALIZATION

We have already pointed out the relevance of data collection to the proper setup and implementation of ChatGPT. We also know that models are pre-trained based on the information and texts that are on the Internet. It is through the analysis of such information that artificial intelligence has the ability to generate content extremely similar to that produced by us humans.

Given the importance of data collection, it is therefore appropriate to devote a paragraph to how it should be carried out and the subsequent customization of the model.

Data collection can be done through manual data-entry. This solution is useful, for example, if you wanted to create a chatbot capable of answering company-related questions such as shipping times, opening hours, or the price of a particular product.

Alternatively, and for more general information, online searches can be conducted. In this case, it is important to check the accuracy of the data collected and ensure that they are relevant and contain enough information to train the model.

After collecting all the data, it is advisable to spend time reviewing them, so as to make sure that they are complete, correct, and there are no repetitions.

Then it is possible to adjust and adapt the model to the business context, adjusting the parameters to improve performance and reduce the error rate. In this sense, it is useful to do experiments with different parameters such as learning rate, number of layers or model size. In addition, it is possible to teach ChatGPT "special" knowledge, such as technical terms, or educate and specialize it in a particular activity or field.

"Fine-tuning" is also a key step in AI customization. In fact, this is a phase in which the model is refined by checking the outputs and verifying their correctness and appropriateness to the context. During this process, it is important to validate the model so as to be sure that it succeeds in achieving the desired results in terms of performance and accuracy. Again, the setting must be continuous and prioritized.

ChatGPT optimization can be carried out by leveraging tools such as error analysis or test models.

A final aspect to consider when customizing an AI tool is that of ethicality. Be sure to include ethical evaluations so that the model cannot negatively impact consumers. This can be done through the inclusion of human reviewers tasked with verifying the content produced by ChatGPT or by implementing rules capable of preventing undesirable outputs.

HOW TO GENERATE A TEXT WITH CHATGPT

One of the most common uses of ChatGPT is the generation of text which, as we saw earlier, can range from creative writing, poetry, short stories, or publishing posts or articles. In order for text to be generated with ChatGPT, it is necessary to provide a "prompt," which is text that the template will use as a starting point for generating new text. The prompt can be a question, a sentence, a paragraph, and so on.

For example, if we wished to generate a short story, we could provide the following prompt to our model: "Once upon a time, in a faraway land, there was a prince who dreamed of exploring the lands far from his kingdom."

The model will use this prompt to generate a short story based on it. The resulting prompt might read, "The young prince then decided to set out on a journey to explore the faraway lands. He traveled through forests and over mountains, encountering many fantastic creatures along the way. Finally he reached a large and opulent city where he met a beautiful princess who was held captive by an evil sorcerer. The prince fought him and freed the princess, living happily ever after with his beloved."

From this example, it is easy to see how ChatGPT is able to generate text that is coherent and capable of following a logical time frame. It represents only one example of how ChatGPT can be used in the field of text creation.

Another area where this tool is used is in answering questions, especially in the area of customer service, chatbots, or virtual assistants. Here ChatGPT can be used to answer questions based on the context provided. Therefore, to set up the model correctly, a context and a question must be provided. For example, you can provide the following context: "Rome is the capital of Italy"; thus, when asked

"What is the capital of Italy?" the model will provide the answer "Rome."

Whether you are a writer, copywriter, marketing manager, researcher or professional, ChatGPT can help you create high-quality content that will engage your intended audience and help you achieve your goals.

THE IMPORTANCE OF PROMPTS IN CHATGPT

To fully understand the potential of ChatGPT, it is critical to understand the role of prompts in the content creation process.

The term prompt, in fact, refers to a set of instructions or guidelines provided to ChatGPT so that the latter can deliver high-quality, goal-focused results. The careful and meticulous setting of prompts, therefore, becomes a key step in getting the artificial intelligence to deliver content in line with the brand's tone of voice and targeted to the target audience.

In addition, effective use of prompts means that large-scale content can be produced in less time, easing the burden of publishing for activities such as e-commerce, media agencies, or social media platforms. Reducing the time to spend on these activities translates into more energy that can be invested in other core business areas.

Having delved into the benefits of using prompts, it is important to note that their quality will have a direct impact on the quality of the content that will be generated by ChatGPT. This means that it is crucial to carve out the necessary time to create prompts tailored to the specific activity, paying attention and avoiding mistakes.

In general, to create ChatGPT prompts consistent with business needs, the following points should be kept in mind:

- Clarity and conciseness
  ChatGPT prompts should first and foremost be clear and concise: on the one hand, they should provide enough detail to guide the software in generating suitable content; on the other hand, they should not contain too much futile information. In this regard, the use of overly technical or complex language is discouraged, while it is recommended to focus on providing specific and clear instructions.

- Use of specific keywords
  Among the key benefits of ChatGPT prompts is content optimization from an SEO perspective. It follows that in order to get the maximum benefits from this model, it is essential to include specific keywords, as well as phrases that are relevant to the target audience and target industry. This step will enable ChatGPT to create content capable of achieving high rankings in search engines and, as a result, increasing traffic to the web platform.

- Provide examples
  It may be useful to include examples containing the type of content desired. This will enable the software to understand what style and tone of voice to use, creating content in line with the brand's communication style.

- Don't overdo the prompts
  Although prompts are a key weapon in harnessing the full benefits of ChatGPT, as with most things the best path lies in between. On the one hand, it is important to provide enough

detail and information so that the software has the notions it needs to make suitable content. On the other hand, overloading ChatGPT with too much information can be confusing to the software, making it difficult for it to understand the instructions and the desired result.

- Doing tests
  As a general rule, before implementing a new technology, it is recommended that tests be conducted to verify its operation and performance. ChatGPT is no exception, so it is important to test prompts before using them within an initiated marketing campaign.
  This will provide an opportunity to check how the software responds to instructions and make necessary changes before actual implementation.

By following these simple tips, ChatGPT's prompt setting will be effective and useful in improving the quality and engagement of digital and non-digital content.

3.
ARTIFICIAL INTELLIGENCE AND CHATGPT IN THE MARKETING WORLD

After reading the introduction of artificial intelligence and ChatGPT found in the previous pages, it becomes quite intuitive to understand what the benefits of leveraging this technology can be in the marketing sector as well.

BENEFITS OF USING ARTIFICIAL INTELLIGENCE

Before venturing into the specifics of ChatGPT, let us look in detail at what benefits all marketers can gain through the use of artificial intelligence-based software. These tools, in fact, are increasingly taking a prominent role in supporting marketing campaigns and the achievement of positive results. Specifically, key benefits include:

- Quality content creation
  Artificial intelligence-based marketing applications can help businesses generate quality content quickly and efficiently. One example is Copy.ai, which is one of many tools that can offer a wide variety of useful templates and prompts to support professionals and provide editing tools.
  Using artificial intelligence to create content of various kinds also saves time and produces more text. Another element of primary importance is that AI-produced content tends to be more consistent because it is created using algorithms

designed specifically to be in line with the brand's style and tone of voice.

This makes this solution particularly effective in business settings where a large amount of content needs to be produced on a regular basis.

- Designing customized marketing campaigns

  Programs like Jasper are an example of how artificial intelligence can help businesses in creating personalized marketing campaigns based on customer behavior and data. By analyzing this information, marketers have the ability to create campaigns that are more targeted and, as a result, more relevant to their target audience. As all marketers know, this translates into more effective campaigns.

  In recent years, personalization, especially in marketing, has become increasingly central, leading consumers to expect messages and offers tailored to them and their interests. In this context, artificial intelligence becomes an essential piece in responding to customer needs by creating customized campaigns that can pander to consumers' expectations and build a stronger relationship with them.

- SEO optimization of content

  There are many applications, such as Writesonic, that use artificial intelligence technology to generate content for websites or social media that is of excellent quality and, most importantly, SEO-optimized.

  These are ideal solutions for improving indexing and generating more traffic on business platforms. Indeed, it is well known that SEO is increasingly a nodal point for all businesses that wish to attract more consumers online, as better indexing often results in more online traffic and more sales.

By leveraging AI to optimize digital content, companies can secure texts in line with SEO best practices and increase the chances of online visibility and sales.

- Automation of marketing processes

  Nowadays, there are many artificial intelligence-based alternatives that offer tools for marketing automation and to support companies in saving time and resources.

  One example is Copysmith, software that offers tools for scheduling and automating posts to be published on social media. Mutiny AI, on the other hand, represents an alternative for all professionals who wish to streamline the process of sending newsletters or other marketing emails. This feature is particularly useful in companies that have to manage and organize large volumes of marketing activities, making the process more streamlined and reducing the constant tasks that marketers are subjected to.

- Data analysis and report creation

  Many AI applications offer advanced data analysis and reporting tools, providing valuable support for businesses that need to track and measure the performance of their marketing campaigns.

  These are tools capable of providing detailed insights and insights focused on verifying the effectiveness and efficiency of different communication channels, as well as of the performance of different types of digital content or the behavior and preferences of each segment of the target audience.

Making this process automatic means saving a great deal of time and, on the other hand, having the opportunity to be more aware of the results and marketing activities best suited to the specific business.

In general, AI-based applications can be an extremely powerful and efficient tool in supporting businesses in the creation and distribution of high-quality content. Due to their structure, they save time and resources, as well as ensure better results in marketing campaigns. As the use of artificial intelligence in this area continues to grow, it is crucial that businesses and professions stay abreast of the latest updates as they begin to consider possible areas of use for this promising new technology.

CRITICAL POINTS OF ARTIFICIAL INTELLIGENCE

Although the advantages presented in the preceding lines undoubtedly represent a turning point in the marketing and communications industry, there are critical points that should be taken into account when considering incorporating artificial intelligence-based technology into one's business. Important points of attention include:

- Content verification
  One of the biggest challenges professionals face when integrating an AI program into their business is content verification.
  Although artificial intelligence can generate extremely good content, some editing and proof-reading may be necessary to ensure that the text is of the best possible quality. To overcome this critical issue, all professionals should carefully

check the content created through artificial intelligence, making any necessary changes so that the final text is accurate, clear, and consistent with the brand image.

- Managing content
Another challenge that businesses may face after the implementation of AI is the amount of content produced by the software. Through artificial intelligence, in fact, businesses can generate a large volume of content in a rather narrow time frame. This can have positive, but also negative implications: on the one hand, there is the possibility of producing much more text in less time; on the other hand, it could be complicated to manage such a volume of content. Some companies may therefore find it difficult to keep track of all the content generated by artificial intelligence.
To overcome this difficulty, companies might consider implementing a content management system that can help in content organization and analysis. In addition, the introduction of clear and well-defined guidelines that can indicate processes in content management is essential.

- Ensuring privacy and data protection
Very often, companies using AI tools need to collect and process a large amount of personal data. They may include information such as customer demographics, behaviors and preferences. Although such information is essential for creating personalized and targeted marketing campaigns on different segments, it is at the same time crucial that the company ensures that the use of that data is in line with privacy and data protection regulations.
To remedy this issue, companies can consider implementing stricter policies and procedures in data control and privacy,

as well as keeping abreast of the latest regulations issued by Italy or Europe. That said, it is important to lean on AI software that can provide excellent guarantees in the protection of sensitive data and their traceability.

- Cost management

Cost management is a critical issue of no small importance. Although AI tools are an extremely effective element of business development, it is also true that they can be quite costly, especially for businesses that are in their infancy or have limited resources.

This downside can be overcome through a careful and judicious analysis of the budget available, so as to assess how much of it can be allocated to an AI technology and identify the tool best suited to specific business needs. In addition, it is important to consider that many AI programs offer flexible plans that allow users to pay as they need to.

Beyond the actual costs of implementing this technology, one should not underestimate the ROI (return on investment) that a tool of this magnitude will have on business results over the medium to long term.

Although the use of artificial intelligence requires attention points, these critical issues can be overcome through the right strategy and approach. By carefully assessing business needs and goals, each entity will be able to choose the AI marketing tool most in line with its needs and implement it in business processes in a way that maximizes benefits and brings possible drawbacks to a minimum.

THE ROLE OF CHATGPT IN MARKETING

If you are a professional working in the marketing field, you surely know how important it is to create quality content that can engage and interest your target audience. Yet with so many tasks to complete each day, it can be difficult to stay on top of content creation. That's where ChatGPT comes in.

As we know ChatGPT is a template that uses artificial intelligence to generate high-quality text, whether copy, blogs, websites, social media posts or other communication channels. It also uses a wide variety of useful templates and prompts to support users in creating and editing, which are essential elements for anyone working in the marketing industry.

The 5 benefits of ChatGPT in the marketing world can be summarized in the following macro areas:

- Customization
  ChatGPT enables marketers to create customized content and marketing campaigns targeted to customers and their consumption patterns.
  For example, a company selling organic skincare products may use ChatGPT to carry out a marketing campaign targeting middle- to high-income housewives living in residential areas.
  It is a particularly effective tool for businesses that want to build and strengthen the relationship with their customers, improving the conversion of marketing campaigns.

- Rapidity

ChatGPT helps marketers generate quality content more quickly and easily, an extremely useful support in companies where the volume of content to be produced is quite high.

A classic example of this is the launch of a new product, a time when it is necessary to create a lot of specific content in a tight time frame. In this context ChatGPT can become an ally in drafting an efficient communication campaign in a short time.

- Accuracy

Because ChatGPT uses rather advanced NLP, or natural language processing, algorithms, the model is able to generate accurate and relevant content. This feature means that ChatGPT can be used by marketers who wish to reach their target audience more effectively.

For example, a company that wants to target a specific age group or a specific geographic location could use ChatGPT to create content in line with the language or idioms typical of that user group.

- Collaboration

ChatGPT offers collaborative editing tools that allow teams to work together on content reaction. In particular, this feature is extremely useful for maintaining the fluidity of work and saving time.

As a practical example, this model can be used by all members of a marketing team working on the same project, making it easier to collaborate and finish the work.

- Integration

Nowadays, the integration of a tool is essential for its proper use and to exploit its full potential. ChatGPT is no exception and can easily be integrated with popular marketing tools such as Google Analytics or Mailchimp. Such integration supports marketers in monitoring the performance of marketing campaigns and thus making decisions based on timely data analysis.

For example, ChatGPT can monitor the performance of a social media campaign, analyzing the results and checking which posts are most in line with the target audience.

ChatGPT represents a tool with great potential for all people in marketing who want to improve content production, personalize campaigns, or collaborate effectively with other team members. Whatever your role, ChatGPT can help you in working more effectively and efficiently so that you can focus more on achieving your goals.

4.
CREATION OF AN INTEGRATED MARKETING STRATEGY

INTEGRATE MARKETING STRATEGY

In this section we will look at what steps need to be followed to implement an efficient marketing campaign integrated with artificial intelligence.

- Identify the objectives

  Before using any artificial intelligence model, it is important to identify what goals and objectives you want to achieve. What do you hope to achieve with the help of AI? Do you want to generate high-quality copy, do you want to create a targeted marketing campaign? Do you want to analyze your segment data?

  Defining your goals ahead of time will allow you to choose which ChatGPT prompts are most suitable and, possibly, which other AI tools you can include in your plan.

- Check alternatives

  Once you have defined the target you wish to achieve, you need to check what the alternatives are. In the specifics of ChatGPT prompts, it becomes critical to identify those that are most in line with the project and for achieving the target goals. With regard to AI, on the other hand, it might be useful to evaluate other applications on the market and their specific uses. To choose the tool best suited to your needs, it is important to conduct thorough research and compare the features and capabilities of each artificial intelligence software.

Take into consideration elements such as cost, usability, integration with other marketing tools, and reviews from other users. It may be especially useful to compare yourself with other professionals who use AI software, so that you know their views and direct experience with the technology.

- Set up ChatGPT or the AI
  Once the prompts to be used or other AI software to be integrated into the marketing strategy have been chosen, the next step is to set up the models.
  Usually this step requires creating an account, entering business data, marketing information, setting up interest data, and integrating with other marketing tools such as Google Ads. To succeed in these steps, simply follow the instructions provided by ChatGPT or the other AI software when opening the account. If you are not an IT expert, don't worry. Fortunately, most artificial intelligence programs dedicated to marketing have been made with a fairly intuitive interface that can be easily used even by people less familiar with using modern technology.

- Test, test, test
  As soon as ChatGPT or another AI software is ready, it is time to start the testing phase. Use the program's features and capabilities to try to create copy content, marketing campaigns, or analyze data of interest to you.
  Pay attention to the results you get and take the time to review and edit what does not match the desired result. Integrated marketing with AI represents a process of optimization and experimentation, so don't be afraid to try different approaches and experiment until you find what works best for you and your business.

TESTING ARTIFICIAL INTELLIGENCE IN THE MARKETING PLAN

As we have seen in the previous lines, the testing phase is a vital piece in the creation of a well-developed marketing plan in line with the brand. As this is a vitally important moment, there are some tricks to take into account.

First of all, it is important to start with small-scale testing. Don't go overboard and get carried away by doing too many tests. Start gradually and incorporate the use of other tools little by little, after you have become familiar with the basics of the software. That way you will have time to learn and adjust, and avoid feeling overwhelmed by too much information or too many features.

Another essential step in the testing phase is undoubtedly the analysis and tracking of results. At this time you need to pay special attention to marketing outputs, making the best use of analytics and data to check what works and what needs to be improved. Focus on the patterns and trends in your results and use this information to optimize your AI-based marketing tools.

Having an open mind is another aspect that should not be underestimated during the testing phase. The world of artificial intelligence is constantly evolving, which means that new features, new tools and new technologies are being developed every day. Being open to trying out new AI applications dedicated to marketing and testing new approaches will allow you to experiment and discover different techniques and figure out which way is best for your business.

In case you are working together with a team, during the testing phase it is critical to make sure that all team members are aligned and know how to use the features of ChatGPT or other AI software.

Last but not least, ChatGPT and all artificial intelligence programs are most efficient when they are properly integrated within the company's marketing strategy. In this regard, it is essential to think about how AI tools can be incorporated within the strategy, developing a plan in which they are able to support the achievement of objectives. Some practical examples might be creating an editorial plan on social, setting up automated newsletters, or analyzing data to stay up-to-date on consumer trends and behavior patterns.

TIPS FOR INTEGRATING AI INTO STRATEGY

From a practical point of view, integrating artificial intelligence into a marketing plan requires basic steps, which must be carried out with extreme care and attention.

- Identify areas for improvement
  If yours is an established business, carve out some time to analyze what areas marketing could be improved. Those will become the focus where ChatGPT can be particularly helpful. For example, it might emerge that your copy is not effective, that the SEO part can be improved, or that your content is not properly targeted.

- Developing an AI marketing plan
  Once areas for improvement have been identified, it is time to develop an integrated marketing plan with AI. Think about the potential of ChatGPT and how it can be used to make

marketing campaigns more effective at the weak points highlighted in the previous step. For example, if your copy is not effective, you could focus your energies on learning how to use ChatGPT to create engaging, high-quality content.

- Putting the target at the center
  Sometimes it can happen that the euphoria of experimentation leads to forgetting fundamental aspects. For this reason, as you develop your marketing plan, do not leave your target audience in the background. Always consider the needs, interests and behaviors of your audience and use this information to create marketing campaigns on the same wavelength as them.

- Verify the results
  Analyzing and verifying results is always an essential part of marketing. In order for you to get the most out of ChatGPT, make sure you never neglect this stage. Even when you are satisfied with your results. It is only through constant analysis that you can make timely changes when required. In addition, analysis allows you to keep up with the trends and behavior patterns of the segment.

- Continuous optimization
  This phase actually represents a natural consequence of the results audit. In fact, careful and timely analysis makes it possible to optimize the marketing plan and secure positive results in the medium to long term.
  In addition, the fields of artificial intelligence and marketing are both extremely dynamic, so it is crucial to approach them with flexibility. Only in this way will it be possible to achieve results that are relevant and suitable for the specific activity.

- Organizing trainings
  Should you have a team dedicated to marketing, make sure that all members are able to make the best use of ChatGPT and other AI tools. With this in mind, it can be particularly useful to organize training or introduction programs to the software that can include documentation, tutorials, shadowing, or 1-to-1 training to improve the use of AI.

- Establish processes and protocols
  To ensure that AI-based marketing tools are in line with the brand's communication strategy, it is essential to establish processes and protocols that are tasked with defining the use of such applications. This category may include guidelines for content creation, internal processes for text approval, or specific quality control measures.

Once the marketing plan has been drafted, collaboration with the team remains paramount. For this reason, it is important to encourage all team members to use ChatGPT and communicate any doubts or concerns about the program. In addition, since it is an evolving software, it is critical to stay abreast of innovations, new features, or improvements applied to it. In this regard, you can consider attending conferences on the topic, signing up for online courses, or reading industry blogs.

Finally, the ethical implications of artificial intelligence should not be overlooked. Among the most perplexing factors are issues related to privacy and content accuracy. Be aware of these limitations when using AI-based marketing tools and make sure you use them responsibly and ethically.

EMAIL MARKETING WITH CHATGPT

In this section we will discover together some practical examples on how to leverage ChatGPT's technology to get personalized emails in no time.

- Generating newsletters for subscribers based on their interests or past purchases.
  Sample prompt: "Write the text of a personalized email to a customer who recently purchased a hiking backpack, including tips for upcoming purchases and special offers."

- Writing copy capable of persuading newsletter subscribers to take a specific action.
  Sample prompt: "Write copy for an email promoting a limited offer on a popular product, including a strong call-to-action."

- Creation of specific email templates with different types of messages, such as newsletter, promotional, or non-empty carts.
  Example prompt: "Write the text of an email for an abandoned shopping cart, also include a personalized message and a special offer.

- Implementation of an automated email sequence with the goal of converting prospects into customers.
  Sample prompt: "Write the text of three emails to automate a new subscriber campaign for a wellness company. Include a welcome email and an email with buying tips.

- Generate an information-oriented email campaign with a goal of conversion over time.

Sample prompt: "Write the text of five emails for a communications campaign for an IT company. The target audience is small business owners; also include useful tips and ideas for using the product."

- Create a newsletter to update and engage subscribers.
  Sample prompt: "Write the text of a cooking blog newsletter, include recipe ideas and a special offer."

- Crafting a useful email to convert clicks and maximize ROI.
  Sample prompt: "Write the text of an email dedicated to Black Friday discounts. Include a strong value proposition, social proof and a clear call-to-action."

- Find ideas for an email campaign that will engage subscribers and increase conversions.
  Sample prompt: "Find five ideas for an email campaign for a clothing store dedicated to women in their 20s and 30s."

- Craft an email for a specific segment of the target audience.
  Sample prompt: "Write the text of an email for a fitness company. The target audience is gym newbies; also include personalized advice and special offers."

- Write catchy headlines to increase email open rates.
  Sample prompt: "Write the title of 10 emails for a company that sells cosmetics. Use friendly language and create a sense of urgency in the reader."

- Suggestions on products to be included in personalized offers in a newsletter.

Sample prompt: "What products would you recommend to a person who is interested in outdoor sports?"

OPTIMIZE SEO WITH CHATGPT

All marketers recognize the essential value of a well-done SEO (Search Engine Optimization) and the large amount of time this activity requires for the results to be effective. This is where ChatGPT comes in with its ability to simplify this process, support in keyword research, meta-description writing and other SEO-related tasks.

In the next few lines you will find some useful practical examples to give you an idea of how ChatGPT can support you in this delicate and crucial step of a marketing strategy.

- Keyword search
  Sample prompt: "Write a list of 10 keywords with high search volume and interest for a blog post about sustainable food consumption."

- Writing titles and descriptions
  Sample prompt: "Write a meta-title and description for a website dedicated to selling organic gardening products."

- Content optimization
  Sample prompt: "SEO-optimize the content of a blog post devoted to the benefits of physical activity."

- Header tags realization
  Example prompt: "Write H1, H2 and H3 tags for a blog post about the benefits of yoga, creating links to products on the site.

- XML site map creation
  Sample prompt: "Write an XML sitemap for a website dedicated to selling organic beauty products."

- Identification tags
  Sample prompt: "Write a list of tags for a website dedicated to selling eco-friendly household products."

- Identifying alt tags
  Example prompt: "Add alt tags to images featured in a blog post devoted to the benefits of artificial intelligence."

- Social media optimization
  Sample prompt: "SEO-optimize social media posts promoting climbing products."

- Data analysis
  Example prompt: "Set up analytics for a website selling organic beauty products and monitor performance."

5.
SOCIAL MEDIA MARKETING AND ARTIFICIAL INTELLIGENCE

After reading the previous chapters, you have surely understood how artificial intelligence is helping us to make our daily lives and work easier.

In this chapter we will explore the close link between social media and artificial intelligence and how both can prove to be a trump card for companies capable of using the best of both technologies.

THE LINK BETWEEN SOCIAL MEDIA AND AI

The concept behind artificial intelligence is based on an algorithm that attempts to recreate the thinking patterns of humans to complete the tasks submitted. To do this, AI needs a constant supply of high-quality data.

Isn't this process similar to that of the much popular social media? In fact, social media would not exist if it were not for artificial intelligence. In fact, many characteristic aspects of social networks are based on this technology. One example is Instagram, where the platform used to recommend profiles to follow based on the feed or the list of followers/following. The same algorithm is behind the product recommendations that appear on Amazon's homepage. In this case, artificial intelligence analyzes user behavior on the platform and leverages the results to find content that might interest them. This technology causes users to spend more and more time on social platforms, thereby increasing the engagement rate and user experience.

Many social media platforms also use artificial intelligence as a tool to detect possible abuse in comment sections and posts. Facebook, for example, uses an artificial intelligence tool known as deep text to detect such situations. According to Facebook, the ultimate goal of this technology is to build a system with the same level of intelligence as a human being.

Yet in recent years it is not only social media platforms that are using AI. In fact, more and more registered users of social channels are taking advantage of this technology for their own personal gain. Nowadays, there are even AI influencers, that is, non-human influencers based on artificial intelligence. One example is Lil Miquela, an AI influencer described as a "19-year-old robot living in Los Angeles." The account actually represents a clever marketing stunt by Brud, a Los Angeles-based startup. Through this idea, Miquela has managed to reach more than 3 million followers.

Nowadays, there is no denying the importance of social media for businesses. More than half of the world, about 58 percent, has at least one social media profile. This figure makes social channels the largest focus group on the planet, as well as a potentially endless pool of customers.

Despite the great potential of this communication channel, keeping up with the demand for content is not always easy: you have to think of new topics that can turn into interesting posts, you have to post at the right times to get good visibility or use the right hashtags to reach the target audience of interest. On social media, there are so many variables that come into play to create an effective communication strategy. And this is precisely where artificial intelligence can step in.

In fact, this technology can help all social media marketing and communications professionals improve performance on this important digital channel, regardless of whether they are in the office or doing remote work.

THE BENEFITS OF THE AI IN SOCIAL MEDIA MARKETING

Having understood the close link between social media and artificial intelligence, it is useful to go into detail about the most important benefits this technology can bring to social media marketers.

- Easier customization

Generic content is now out of step with the digital world, and users increasingly want content that looks like it was created specifically for them. This is even more true when searching for new products to purchase. Many customers expect offers to be tailored to them based on their interactions with the brand, site, or similar content. This widespread expectation among Internet users means that personalization has become an essential element in digital communication strategies.

Of course, personalizing content is not that simple, and it is nearly impossible to personalize a post for every single customer on social media. Instead, the goal should be to engage as many people as possible at once through content that is relevant to followers.

Many companies rely on market research on the target audience to create customized content. Now, this is not a wrong process as market research can always prove useful, however, today we can go further. In fact, thanks to social media, we have at our disposal a real treasure trove consisting of the data of users registered to the different platforms. Such data gives us access to the behaviors and interests of each follower. This is where artificial intelligence can enhance social media communication.

There is a specific system for predicting content popularity and using artificial intelligence to analyze and understand customers and their behavior patterns. Through the analysis of this information, the system can recommend the type of content that would be of interest to followers. Anyone working in the marketing industry can easily realize the potential of such a tool, which can cut out the hours and hours spent thinking about the most suitable content and the most suitable editorial plan for digital channels. Today, to know what the audience wants, it is enough to take advantage of artificial intelligence.

Of course, this information has enormous potential that is not just limited to social media. For example, this enhancement can affect content creation for any communication channel and could mean more effective emails or more interactive and engaging content on the website.

- Discovering customer value

  Although the idea that people have value might seem a bit dystopian, it is a concept that is critical to focus on when you want to succeed in business.

  Customer Lifetime Value (CLV) indicates the amount of monetary value customers will bring to the business during their relationship with the brand. It represents critical information for all marketing professionals. After all, from a remunerative point of view, it makes no sense to spend money and resources chasing customers with low expected monetary value. On the other hand, this indicator is not static and can be increased over time. However, to succeed in this endeavor, it is necessary to be present at every stage of the relationship with a customer, improving his or her experiences in relation to the brand. The more positively a customer views a brand, the longer they will spend their hard-earned money with it.

In this sense, artificial intelligence in social media can become an enabler for both aspects of Customer Lifetime Value.

By getting more and more followers, the total number of potential customers can be increased. Artificial intelligence can then analyze the habits of followers to predict their CLV more accurately. The technology is also useful when you want to increase a customer's CLV by providing information on how to improve their experience.

To improve experiences with the brand, it is important to make sure that you build a very good quality website. Otherwise, people will not stay on the site after clicking on a post. For this reason, it is advisable to choose the right web hosting services and keep the website up-to-date.

- Content planning

Artificial intelligence enables social media professionals to achieve more in less time. Examples include repetitive tasks such as publishing and content planning, which can be automated to allow professionals to focus on strategy and activities that can generate increased ROI.

Automated content scheduling also makes social media posts much more efficient and scalable. Thanks to artificial intelligence, posts on multiple platforms can be scheduled simultaneously. Not to mention that many such tools also offer detailed analytics to monitor the performance of individual marketing campaigns.

In addition, automating the creation of new and engaging content and speeding up the analysis of its performance allows relevant content to be republished in the optimal engagement timeframe.

Republishing content can include historical posts or curated content from relevant accounts and channels that audiences will find interesting. The integration of artificial intelligence and social media makes the content curation process much faster and more effective.

- Faster interactions

  Manually interacting with followers, retweeting, sharing, or finding authentic answers to comments and questions can be an extremely time-consuming and demanding task. However, there are artificial intelligence-based tools capable of making this process much faster and easier.

  For example, there are AI programs that can analyze brand-related conversation and present marketers with a list of tweets that could be retweeted to encourage customer loyalty, engagement, and brand advocacy. The results can even be filtered to remove posts that include words, links or comments that you do not want associated with your brand.

  Customers also often use social media to reach out quickly and expect someone on the other end who can respond with quick and relevant messages. Nearly 65 percent of consumers expect a brand to respond to a question on social media within 24 hours. This highlights quite strongly the expectations users have of brands on social platforms.

In this regard, AI-based chatbots can provide great help, leveraging natural language processing (NLP) to be present with quick and consistent answers to consumer questions or customer service queries on social channels. When the request is too complex, artificial intelligence can forward the query to human "colleagues" in customer service.

- More intuitive post tracking
  We all know that social media campaigns generate a large amount of data, so much that it can sometimes be excessive.
  Artificial intelligence intervenes by making the process of data analysis and information capture much faster and more intuitive. There are analytics tools that can simplify social media reporting by showing all of the social channel analytics in an intuitive and easy to interpret dashboard. This allows you to see the number of impressions, likes, shares, as well as the reach of your own social media posts and those of competitors' accounts. Finally, artificial intelligence can show when the target audience is most active and the best days and times for good engagement performance.

- Measuring performance with ease
  The success of a social media campaign depends on having the right information at the right time. Nowadays there are AI-based tools on the market that can support marketers in keeping track of user engagement, follower counts, impressions, competitor benchmarks and much more.
  Again, data are displayed in a single dashboard that can be quickly accessed for insights and to identify areas for improvement. Of course, performance metrics can be customized or created from scratch to get the data needed to verify personal KPIs.

Then there are AI tools that can obtain information about competitors' strategy and performance without having to resort to time-consuming manual research or reporting. This provides an opportunity to observe competitors' social activities and create a benchmark to compare performance on social channels. Some of these tools are integrated with social listening functionality, so you can learn what consumers think about competitors' products and services. With this information, it is easier to identify the best ways to differentiate the brand.

Social listening can also be leveraged to gain insights from the vast number of conversations on social media platforms through keywords, hashtags, competitors, and so on. Monitoring these terms can reveal unfiltered information about brand perception and how people use products and services. Brands can use this information for many different areas ranging from editorial plans to research and development.

Artificial intelligence represents both the future and the present of social media. Already, machine learning, automation and analytics based on artificial intelligence functions are helping marketers make sense of the enormous amount of data that social media creates and put this information to use to improve business performance.

In addition, as consumer expectations are higher than ever, brands need to leverage AI to be present with the right messages at the right time and on the right platform. With this new technology, marketers have the ability to use information gained from customer data to create strategy and react quickly to new trends in consumer behavior.

DISADVANTAGES OF AI IN SOCIAL MEDIA MARKETING

Despite the many benefits of artificial intelligence applied to social media marketing, it is essential to also evaluate the cons of this technology before integrating it into digital activities.

- Quality issues and possible plagiarism

  Because artificial intelligence relies on data and algorithms to create content, there may be quality issues. Artificial intelligence tools, in fact, can cover the black or white areas of a topic; the gray areas are more subjective and therefore more complicated for an AI tool to address.

  In addition, search engines might flag a piece of content because it is too similar to previously published materials or sources that artificial intelligence has drawn on to produce the content.

  Basically, artificial intelligence tools gather content from various websites and reformulate it to get the final output. Without adding the correct flow, this process could go against Google's guidelines regarding "merging and combining content."

  It should also be kept in mind that the content must be authoritative and informative, which can be difficult to achieve when piecing together information from various online sites without proper human review.

- Algorithms devalue content

  Google released a content update in August 2022; it highlights the following: "useful content written by people, for people." In the update, Google emphasized that the search engine looks for content made by people. The update thus seems to punish content created solely for the purpose of ranking higher in search results. Since many artificial intelligence tools evaluate SEO results first at the expense of actual text comprehension, it follows, according to Google, that AI results are focused on keywords and are not truly informative to the reader.

- Lack of creativity and customization
  Creative content makes articles more engaging for users, so much so that people tend to share more articles for which they feel a connection. However, artificial intelligence does not yet have the emotional intelligence to create a story, but merely adds the facts or information to a communication pattern.
  Also, relying on data contained on websites, it may not understand the user's intent or expectations, thus failing to provide responses in line with emotional or common sense behaviors.

- Human control is needed
  Despite the many steps forward, marketers still need to read content generated by artificial intelligence. So while it might save some time, people still need to be involved in the process and the quality of articles should always be checked.
  This is because AI tools combine information found online into a single text, so there may be some errors to correct. Examples are product descriptions as some AI tools do not fully understand the meaning of adjectives.

- It is not possible to generate new ideas
  Artificial intelligence tools use existing information to make content, which means they do not have the ability to find new ideas or create original content. In addition, if it is an

innovative and still unfamiliar field, it can be complicated to generate content with the support of artificial intelligence because of the paucity of information available online.

6.
INTEGRATING ARTIFICIAL INTELLIGENCE INTO SOCIAL MEDIA

Making a successful campaign on social channels such as Instagram or Facebook requires a lot of planning, testing and optimization. In this process, artificial intelligence can become an important weapon because of the support it can provide on different aspects.

In any case, the advice given for integrating artificial intelligence within the marketing strategy also applies to social channels, as there are still points of attention that should not be underestimated.

USE THE AI ON FACEBOOK AND INSTAGRAM

Before proceeding with the practical integration of artificial intelligence-based programs, it is essential to keep a few tips in mind.

- Devote time and attention to configuration
  As we know, tools based on artificial intelligence need specific training from humans before they can achieve the best results.
  Thinking about and planning in advance the content you want to make with artificial intelligence will ensure that you get great content in line with your brand's goals and tone of voice.

- Verify quality before publication

Remember that published content only helps your brand if it has good enough quality to rank well in search engines and provide real value to your readers.

Although artificial intelligence tools can support and help you for most of the work, human review is always necessary to make sure you achieve the desired result in the best way possible.

This is why AI-based content creation tools cannot really replace competent copywriters. On the contrary, AI supports content writers in working more efficiently, taking care of the more mundane aspects of the creation process and enabling copywriters to use their skills to refine content and achieve the best result.

- Mutual education

  Training on content developed by artificial intelligence can be understood as a two-way street. As AI tools learn from you, you must also learn from them.

  For example, you can make your communication strategy more targeted through lessons learned from artificial intelligence tools embedded in marketing. In fact, this technology can do a better job of collecting and analyzing data on user behavior than we humans can.

  Pay attention to posts developed by artificial intelligence: you may discover new keywords, sentence structures, or even more effective call-to-actions.

- Do not rely exclusively on artificial intelligence-generated content

  Any content that expresses a strong opinion or tells a personal story must be written by a real person, although artificial intelligence-based content moderation tools can be used to help with editing and revising tone of voice.

Although ideally AI content should come across as content created by a human, sometimes users and followers may want to read something more personal from your brand.

Human stories help build a connection based on emotion and empathy, both of which are powerful tools for strengthening brand connection. Use artificial intelligence tools to give copywriters more time to create human stories that excite and engage users.

3 WAYS TO INTEGRATE AI INTO SOCIAL STRATEGY

Implementing artificial intelligence in social media strategy is easier than it may seem. In fact, nowadays there are so many AI-based tools that can be leveraged to make social media communication more efficient.

In the next few pages we will discover three ways to incorporate artificial intelligence into social media communication planning.

- Using AI to create simple content and posts

  All professionals have one main enemy: time. Many struggle to find time to record viral videos or create detailed Instagram stories, others spend hours pondering how to write a post that can communicate everything while staying under a certain word count.

  Although artificial intelligence cannot yet write complete blog posts, it can be useful in creating content for social media.

  Some artificial intelligence tools can recognize context from broader content and create social media posts to promote it. In addition to this, there are AI tools with dashboards and other functions related to planning and managing social media projects. They also can analyze historical reports and recommend the best posting times for maximum impact.

Notable programs in this area include HubSpot, a program capable of automatically creating social posts based on the metadata of the link that was copied and pasted. After entering the post's attachments, such as the URL, you will see a short title or meta description of the page along with its link and a photo. Finally, you can schedule the content to be published at the desired time.

- Monitor and analyze channels
Writing content and providing prompt responses are only half the battle that every social media manager faces while managing social media. A huge part of marketing on this digital channel, in fact, is managing and continuously monitoring social channels.

Fortunately, today artificial intelligence can take on a good portion of this work and help you make better marketing decisions in the process. That's because artificial intelligence can collect data from millions of posts, at scale, and use that data to make predictions and decisions.

Managing a social channel is quite a complex job, but some of these tasks such as discovering interesting influencers and completing audience analysis can be handled by AI-based tools such as Socialbakers. It is an AI-based social media management platform that can provide detailed audience information, discover potential influencer marketing, and use an intelligent monitoring and planning dashboard.

Then there are other tools with the ability to analyze historical reports and provide recommendations on when and how often to publish based on the data collected, while also generating detailed analyses of key competitors.

Finally, Linkfluence's Radarly software is useful for professionals who need support in evaluating the millions of pieces of data that social media audiences produce every day. This translates into measuring your brand's impact, detecting online trends, and gaining specific insights into your target audience.

- Create, optimize and manage social media ads

  As mentioned earlier, artificial intelligence is able to develop social media posts and optimize it to get as many clicks and conversions as possible by leveraging AI predictive technology.

  For example, Phrasee has developed technology that does just that for short-form advertising text for use on platforms such as Facebook and Instagram. The program pulls data from past marketing assets, including emails, social media copy, and other online posts to determine what content will be effective.

  Starting with this analysis, the program can show you which aspects of past ads were weak or strong. You can then draft new copy and test its effectiveness or use the content suggested by the software itself.

  Then there are artificial intelligence tools that can handle some of the most important tasks in post management, such as optimizing bids, breaking down a budget, or identifying which social channels are most likely to improve the performance of your ad.

IMPLEMENT CHATGPT IN FACEBOOK AND INSTAGRAM POSTS

To help you fully understand the potential of ChatGPT in creating effective posts for Facebook and Instagram, on the next few pages we will look at some practical examples for implementing this technology in your daily social media marketing activities.

- Creating a carousel of images
  ChatGPT can help you generate a list of 10 eye-catching photos capable of attracting your audience.
  Sample prompt: "Write a list of 10 eye-catching and relevant photos to create a Facebook carousel for an interior design company."

- Identify the right target audience for your ads
  AI can be useful in identifying a well-defined target audience for your Facebook and Instagram posts.
  Example prompt: "Write a list of 10 audience segments to get highly targeted and relevant Facebook ads for a travel agency."

- Ideas for new tests
  ChatGPT can be useful in case you want to come up with some innovative new ideas for social channels.
  Sample prompt: "Write a list of 10 innovative, data-driven ideas for testing Facebook ads for an e-commerce business."

- Set clear goals
  Artificial intelligence can help you set clear, measurable goals.

Sample prompt: "Write a list of 10 clear and measurable goals for an Instagram advertising campaign carried out by a company selling women's shoes."

- New targeting strategies for social media
  AI can also be used to create targeted and effective strategies for targeting the target audience.
  Sample prompt: "Write a list of 10 effective, customized targeting strategies to use on Instagram for a company that sells natural beauty products."

7.
HOW THE AI WILL CHANGE THE FUTURE OF MARKETING

Because we live in a time when markets are constantly evolving, artificial intelligence still represents an unclear technology for most people. Moreover, since it is a fairly recent innovation, it is still difficult to predict with certainty what implications it will bring to the world and, more specifically, to the marketing sector.

TOMORROW'S POSSIBLE BENEFITS
In the next few pages we will try to analyze what the future of artificial intelligence within the marketing world might look like.

- Content creation
The secret of successful marketing is not only about finding and reaching customers, but also about reaching them with the right message at the right time. This is where artificial intelligence becomes important because of its precision in data analysis, which is necessary to capture the customer's attention. This will definitely be one of the functions that AI will focus on the most.

- Predictive analysis
Predictive analytics can be applied to data organized from social media or the web to create a better product or service. With increasing technological innovations, artificial intelligence can successfully predict changes in digital

marketing to improve the advertising campaign. It can already process millions of trends and social media posts and find similarities in the texts, images and even hashtags used. This will enable marketers to adapt quickly whenever there is a change in market behavior, improving brand performance.

- Best ads
  According to Garter Analysis, within the next five years, 50 percent of analytical decisions will be made through simple verbal interaction. Unlike traditional approaches to marketing, AI-generated marketing will therefore enable companies to adapt to these changes more smoothly. In addition, AI could play an increasingly important role in the growth of start-ups, enabling them to explore various opportunities with ease.

- Product recommendations
  Product recommendations are one of the most common uses of AI in digital marketing. Its presence has expanded in most industries due to its great growth benefits. Further development of this technology will enable artificial intelligence to learn more and more about users' preferences and put before their eyes the product that perfectly matches their preferences.
  This will not only help you create better content, but also increase your chances of conversion.

- Better customer service
  In digital marketing, one of the important aspects of achieving success is to accurately understand customer behavior and needs. In this field, artificial intelligence is beginning to play an important role in taking customer

service to the next level. It can, in fact, quickly identify and adapt to the pattern of customer information, including past purchase history, preferences and more. As this technology develops, AI will be able to increasingly stimulate customer engagement in real and impactful ways. By communicating positively with potential customers, the entire sales process and customer service will become increasingly smooth and efficient.

- Marketing with augmented and virtual reality
  Augmented and virtual reality marketing modes have been in use for some time, but they are still considered a novelty among consumers. However, in the future, these innovative technologies will not only dominate the world of entertainment, but will also be used in the practical application of marketing.
  Nowadays, we can see that more and more companies are embracing this technology, realizing how much of a positive impact it can have on marketing strategy. For example, some furniture stores are allowing their customers to "try on" their chosen furniture in their homes in the virtual world before purchasing them in the real world. Similarly, several fashion brands are creating apps for customers to try on different alternatives in the comfort of their homes.
- Voice search
  The world is increasingly moving to mobile devices, and virtual assistants based on artificial intelligence are growing dramatically. According to a recent survey, about 60 percent of customers prefer to use voice search to find information about a business, while half implement voice search to identify the business that meets their needs. AI technology is designed to understand human language using machine

learning algorithms. For example, Google's algorithms have been shown to recognize human language with an accuracy rate of 95 percent, similar to the intellectual level of another human being.

- Automated decision making
  There are many challenges to overcome when it comes to making marketing decisions. For example, to implement the best strategy, it is necessary to understand the specific needs, wants, and behaviors of customers. It is also crucial to change the desires or needs of consumers and direct them to your brand.
  With the development of artificial intelligence and simulation techniques in digital marketing, reliable insights into your customers' characteristics will be possible in the future. This process will help predict an individual's behavior and support decisions through the collection of up-to-date, real-time data, analysis of the latest trends and forecasts.

- Dynamic pricing model
  The dynamic pricing model benefits customers and companies when demand for a product or service is declining. Thus, the role of artificial intelligence in pricing strategy involves product pricing based on supply and demand.
  In the future, a chatbot in an app or website may perform predictive analytics through cookies, history, searches, and other activities to provide you with real-time prices. For example, in the case of unoccupied hotel rooms, dynamic pricing could offer competitive prices compared to other competitors to attract more customers.

In short, artificial intelligence is here to stay, but it is still evolving. What we do know is that its growth will lead to sure improvements and its increasing integration into the marketing process, helping marketers to be more effective.

Eventually companies and marketers will benefit a great deal from artificial intelligence and its incredible capabilities. But how long will this take? And what will the future of human-machine collaboration in the marketing world hold?

Unfortunately, we are not able to get these answers today; all we can do is wait, watch and stay on top of things.

CONCLUSION

In this book, we explored the many ways in which a business and its marketing strategy can be improved through the use of artificial intelligence and ChatGPT. From content creation to precise target segmentation, AI-based marketing can offer great benefits and enable professionals to save time, improve efficiency, and achieve higher-performing results.

Nevertheless, it is important to remember that artificial intelligence represents a relatively new technology and therefore there are still many unknown and unexplored aspects. Because it is an ever-evolving field, it is critical that companies are informed, eager to experiment, and ready to seize the opportunities and challenges that lie in the world of AI.

Hopefully, this book has provided you with some useful information and insights to explore and put into practice some of the applications of artificial intelligence in your daily marketing activities.

We are confident that after reading this handbook you will be able to identify the right tools, create the right strategies and maintain an open mindset that will enable you to take your marketing to the next level and achieve all the goals you set for yourself.

Made in the USA
Monee, IL
16 September 2024

65940439R00039